PINWHEEL
Party

12 FUN AND UNIQUE QUILTS

ELLEN PAHL

Martingale®
& COMPANY

DEDICATION

To my grandmothers—Elizabeth Ross, who inspired me to make quilts, and Hazel Codding, who encouraged me in everything I did—and to my mother, Annabelle Stoker, who taught me the art of making do.

Pinwheel Party: 12 Fun and Unique Quilts
© 2010 by Ellen Pahl

That Patchwork Place® is an imprint of
Martingale & Company®.

Martingale & Company
20205 144th Ave. NE
Woodinville, WA 98072-8478 USA
www.martingale-pub.com

CREDITS

President & CEO: Tom Wierzbicki
Editor in Chief: Mary V. Green
Managing Editor: Tina Cook
Developmental Editor: Karen Costello Soltys
Technical Editor: Laurie Baker
Copy Editor: Melissa Bryan
Design Director: Stan Green
Production Manager: Regina Girard
Illustrator: Adrienne Smitke
Cover & Text Designer: Stan Green
Photographer: Brent Kane

Printed in China
15 14 13 12 11 10   8 7 6 5 4 3 2 1

Library of Congress Cataloging-in-Publication Data is available upon request.

ISBN: 978-1-56477-987-8

MISSION STATEMENT

Dedicated to providing quality products and service to inspire creativity.

CONTENTS

Introduction

Pinwheels bring to mind the spring days of my childhood when my mother would fashion a pinwheel from a square of paper, stick it into the eraser end of a pencil with a tack or pin, and blow on it to check its spinning potential. Then she would send me outside to run around and watch it catch the wind.

Now I love to incorporate that spinning pinwheel image into quilts. If you look through Barbara Brackman's *Encyclopedia of Pieced Quilt Patterns* (American Quilters Society, 1993), you'll find no fewer than 27 blocks that are called *Pinwheel* or some variation of Pinwheel. If you look up Windmill, you'll find another 17 blocks plus many other variations on the theme of windmill or wind. Then, of course, there are lots of other blocks that resemble pinwheels or windmills, or that appear to spin and twirl, with names that are totally unrelated.

Obviously, one could fill a huge book with Pinwheel quilts and the block's close cousins. In this book, I've included 12 projects to introduce you to a few of the many variations of the block, from the simplest to some that are a little more complex but still easy to sew. By their very nature, most pinwheel-related blocks include triangles, so I've also provided some tips for working with them. And because most of my quilts are scrappy, I threw in some of my very loose guidelines for choosing colors and fabrics.

The quilts range from small, doll-sized quilts to medium-sized wall hangings. I am enchanted with making small quilts. It allows me to experiment with color, fabric, and various piecing techniques while creating a quilt that doesn't take a long time to complete. These small quilts are wonderful to use in decorating your home—on the walls, on tables and other furniture, rolled up in baskets, or folded and stacked on a child's chair. I always have a small quilt on the kitchen table with a bowl of fruit or bouquet of flowers on top. I change the quilt often to suit the season or mood. These smaller sizes also make super gifts for friends and family.

So, you're officially invited to the pinwheel party. Head to your sewing space, grab your fabric, and give some pinwheels a whirl!

EASIEST PINWHEELS

Pinwheel Pirouette 14

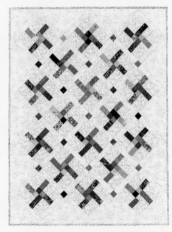

Four-Patch Pinwheels 17

Pinwheel Charm 20

PINWHEELS GROW UP

Nothing but Pinwheels 24

Twice As Nice 27

Windmill Row 31

PINWHEELS PLUS APPLIQUÉ

Three of Hearts 34

Hanging Out 38

Oklahoma Memories 44

NOT YOUR TYPICAL PINWHEELS

Xs and Os 52

Whirlwind 55

Wind Farm 59

Quilting BASICS

There isn't space to cover all the details of quilting in this book. If you're unfamiliar with rotary cutting, machine piecing, or other aspects of quilting, I encourage you to take a class at a local quilt shop or check out some of the many excellent books that cover all aspects of quiltmaking techniques.

To make the quilts in this book, you'll need some essential quiltmaking tools and supplies, a reliable sewing machine, and fabric, of course. You'll also need to be skilled at basic rotary cutting and be able to sew using an accurate ¼" seam allowance.

TOOLS AND SUPPLIES

Essential Items:	Very Helpful Items:
Rotary cutter	12½" x 12½" ruler
Cutting mat	6" x 6" ruler
6" x 24" ruler	Thread snips
Scissors	Half-square ruler
Sewing machine	Quarter-square ruler
Iron	

CHOOSING FABRICS FOR SCRAP QUILTS

I love to make scrap quilts. Years ago, I made a Log Cabin quilt that was double-bed size. Each of the 80 blocks was the same. Each block had several fabrics in it, but I knew in advance what it would look like, and for me, it became somewhat boring to keep making that same block over and over again. Since then, almost every quilt I've made has been scrappy. I like the reward of seeing how the fabrics come together each time I finish a block.

I'm also fond of scrap quilts because they aren't always predictable. This spontaneity is typical of many antique quilts, and I like to imagine how the quilter had to be creative and make do when she ran out of fabric. I follow the philosophy of "making do" as much as possible. Quilts that include some element of surprise for the viewer, whether intentional or not, are often my favorites.

A FEW THOUGHTS ON MAKING SCRAP QUILTS

- Vary the scale, texture, and print as well as the values within your blocks. For example, if you have a tiny dark floral print, balance it with a light geometric print or striped fabric in a larger scale.
- Don't obsess about matching everything perfectly. Sometimes the more unusual combinations turn out to be unexpected winners.
- Don't be afraid to mix contemporary fabrics with reproduction fabrics or mix prints from different lines of fabric. I "shop" in my fabric stash by color and value, not fabric type. Of course, if you want a quilt that resembles an antique quilt, don't add inappropriate fabrics to the mix. But for other quilts, look simply at color, pattern, print scale, and value when choosing fabrics to sew together.
- If you're happy with every block, you will like it when they all come together to make the quilt. However, you don't need to make every block stellar. Some less-outstanding blocks allow your favorites to shine.

Sometimes my quilts have a preconceived color plan and other times not. If there will simply be many colors, I start by choosing and cutting fabrics that I think I might be able to use up, and once in a while, that actually happens! If I have a color plan, for example pinks and browns, I'll go through my stash and pull all the fabrics that I think might be candidates. I include a range of values for each, as well as lots of different prints, scales, and print textures. I also pull some browns that lean toward green, some that might be a purplish brown, and some that are more golden brown. I do the same with the pinks—peachy pinks, brownish pinks, and some that are a bit on the lavender side.

I choose fabrics for several blocks and then cut them out, keeping the pieces for each block together in a stack. As I complete each block, I place it on the design wall or arrange it on my sewing table. I enjoy seeing how the fabrics are coming together and being able to evaluate how different colors, values, and prints affect the look of the block. Then I choose fabrics for several more blocks, cut, and sew.

ROTARY CUTTING FOR SCRAP QUILTS

When cutting a few pieces of fabric for individual blocks, it doesn't make sense to start by cutting a strip across the width of your fabric first—unless you want leftover strips for another project. Once I have chosen fabrics for several blocks, I layer two to three different fabrics so that I can cut the pieces for several blocks at a time. I usually don't cut more than three layers at a time, because it's harder to make accurate cuts with too many layers.

Let's say that you need one 3¾" square of pink print for each block you are making, and you want each square to be from a different fabric. Here's the procedure that I follow to make cutting scrappy quilts less time-consuming and more efficient. (Reverse the positioning if you're left-handed.)

1. Press the selected fabrics to remove any wrinkles. You can press just the section of the fabric that you need to cut.

2. Place the largest piece of fabric on your cutting mat first. Place two additional fabric pieces on top of the first, smoothing out each layer and making sure each one is flat and free of wrinkles. Cut off irregular portions of the fabrics as necessary. The bottom edges and the left edges should be loosely aligned and relatively straight.

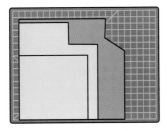

3. For a 3¾" square, I suggest using a 6" or 6½" square ruler. Place the ruler over the fabrics so that it's at least 4" inside the left and bottom edges of all the fabrics. Cut along the right side of the ruler and continue about ⅛" beyond the ruler. Stop cutting, but don't move the ruler. Cut along the top of the ruler to the edge of the fabric.

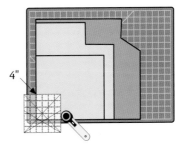

4"

4. Remove the ruler and move the larger pieces of fabric out of the way. You now have a section of layered fabrics, approximately 4" square.

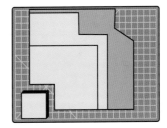

5. Without disturbing the layered fabrics, carefully rotate the section 180° (or rotate your cutting mat). Place the ruler over the fabrics, aligning the 3¾" line with the left and bottom edges. Cut along the right edge of the ruler first and then the top edge to cut your 3¾" squares.

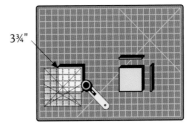

3¾"

Now the squares are ready for piecing, or you can cut them in half or into quarters diagonally to create triangles if required. Use the same technique for rectangles and even short strips of fabric that you want to subcut.

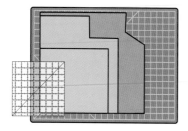

When working with scraps, I often find that I can't cut a large enough square to cut diagonally twice for quarter-square triangles. That's when the quarter-square ruler comes in handy. Many times I can get the triangles I need, even when I couldn't cut a square first. For example, I can't cut a 4¼" square (for 3" finished units) from a 2½" strip, but I can cut four triangles using the ruler. I use a half-square ruler at times too, but less often than the quarter-square ruler. If you have a 2½" strip, you can still cut triangles for a 2" finished half-square-triangle unit. You can cut triangles from random pieces of fabric as well—simply cut a straight edge on uneven or odd-shaped pieces first.

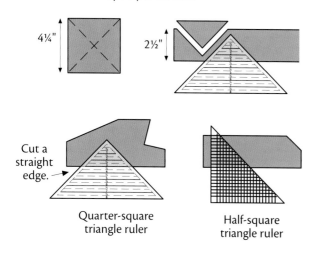

4¼"

2½"

Cut a straight edge.

Quarter-square triangle ruler

Half-square triangle ruler

PIECING POINTERS

Piecing with an accurate ¼" seam allowance will make your quilting life much easier. Of course you need to start out by cutting accurately, and then follow up with careful pressing. Together, accurate cutting, piecing, and pressing will almost guarantee success. Test your seam allowance by sewing two 2" squares together. Press and measure the finished unit. It should measure 2" x 3½". If it doesn't, try again, sewing with a slightly wider or narrower seam allowance as needed.

CHAIN PIECING

I chain piece the units for one or two blocks at a time. When I have sewn all the units for those blocks together and am ready to press them, I take the pieces for a unit from the next block and add them to the chain. Then I cut the chain after the last piece for the first blocks, leaving the unit from the next block under the presser foot. The separated pieces can then be taken to my pressing surface and ironed. Adding the pieces for the next block to the chain gives me a head start on the block and saves thread at the same time. If I don't have any more blocks to piece, I simply sew onto a folded fabric scrap, often referred to as a scrap starter.

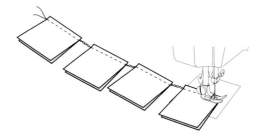

PRESSING TIPS

Pressing is one of the keys to successful piecing. Using steam or not is a personal preference. I usually press with light steam. Always press each seam flat after it has been sewn (with the patches still right sides together) to set the stitches. This helps the sewing thread settle into the threads of the fabric, creating less bulk when the seam allowances are pressed to the side. Press with the fabric that you will be pressing toward on top.

Press with an up-and-down motion, concentrating on the seam. Don't slide the iron over the pieced units, and be especially careful not to distort raw bias edges. Use the tip of your iron to nudge the seam if necessary so that it's nice and flat.

Refer to the diagrams within the step-by-step instructions for each project and press the seam allowances in the direction of the arrows. You can also press seam allowances open, if you prefer, to reduce bulk where several triangle points come together.

HAND APPLIQUÉ

I enjoy needle-turn hand appliqué, but there are many appliqué methods and many variations on each method. Follow the steps in this section for my

SEWING TRIANGLES

Triangles are not difficult, especially if you follow the tips below.

- Always handle triangles gently.

- Once you establish the piecing order, keep each set of triangles positioned the same way as you feed them under the presser foot. It's easy to sew triangles together along the wrong edges—I speak from experience here!

- For quarter-square triangles, always begin sewing from the right-angle corner, and keep the same fabric (either light or dark) on top for each unit that is the same.

- When piecing triangles, trim the points of the seam allowances, often called dog-ears, before pressing. I find it easier to trim them after sewing, when the two layers are still right sides together. I group the pieces, holding them in my left hand like playing cards, and trim the points all at the same time. I keep a wastebasket next

to my sewing table and hold the pieces over it as I trim. Of course, it usually looks like confetti all around because many of the tiny triangles miss the mark, but I like the colorful bits of fabric that surround the basket. It makes it look like someone has been having fun at the sewing machine. Use small, sharp scissors and keep in mind that you're trimming tiny right triangles from each point.

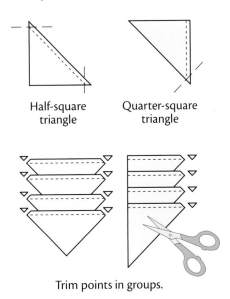

Half-square triangle   Quarter-square triangle

Trim points in groups.

favorite needle-turn method, or use your own preferred technique. I recommend using needles designated for appliqué (sometimes called straw needles), because they are longer and thinner than regular Sharp needles. You might also like to have a round toothpick on hand; you can use it instead of the needle to help turn under the seam allowance.

1. Make a template of the chosen pattern by tracing it onto template plastic or the dull side of a piece of freezer paper. Freezer paper can be reused a few times before it will no longer adhere. Use template plastic if you want a permanent template.

2. If using a freezer-paper template, use your iron to press the shiny side of the template onto the right side of the chosen appliqué fabric. Trace around the freezer paper or plastic template using a pencil or

fabric marker. You want a thin, smooth, and easily visible line. It will be hidden after stitching, so it does not have to be removable.

3. Cut around the shape, a scant ¼" outside the drawn line. Gently remove the freezer paper. (Some people leave it on and use it as a guide for turning under the fabric.)

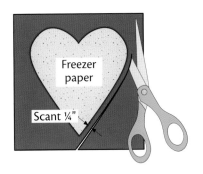

Freezer paper

Scant ¼"

4. Fold the background fabric in half in both directions to create creases that will mark the center both vertically and horizontally. Position the shape(s) on the background fabric and pin in place. Silk pins with small heads are ideal, or use flat-head flower pins. After securing on the front, pin the appliqué shape on the wrong side of the background. Then remove the pins on the right side. This will keep your thread from being caught on the pins as you sew.

5. Cut an 18" to 20" length of thread that matches the appliqué. Thread your appliqué needle and knot one end of the thread. Beginning on a straight side of the shape, bring the needle up through the appliqué from the wrong side of the fabric, just inside the marked line. Pull the needle until the knot rests against the wrong side of the fabric shape. This will hide the knot inside the seam allowance.

6. Fold under the seam allowance, using your needle or a round toothpick to turn it under. Be sure that you have turned under the marked line; crease the fold. Hold the turned-under fold with your left thumb and forefinger. Insert the needle down into the background fabric, next to where the thread emerges from the appliqué fabric. Bring the needle up into the fold of the appliqué fabric, $1/16$" to $1/8$" away. Catch just a couple of threads of the fold and pull the thread taut, but not so tight that the fabric puckers.

7. Turn under more fabric as needed, using a sweeping motion with the toothpick, and repeat the stitching sequence. Note: If you are right-handed, work counterclockwise; left-handers, work clockwise.

8. Continue stitching around the shape. For inner points, clip the V point all the way to the drawn line and turn under the seam allowance. At the V, take two slightly longer stitches into the fabric to hold the threads. Then turn under the next seam allowance, rotate your needle, and continue stitching.

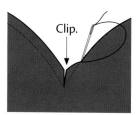

Clip.

For outer points, such as at the bottom of a heart, stitch to the drawn point. Take an extra stitch at the point. Turn the seam allowance back and trim any excess fabric to eliminate bulk. Then sweep the seam allowance under with your toothpick or needle. Tug gently at the last stitch you made to sharpen the point, and continue stitching until you reach the beginning.

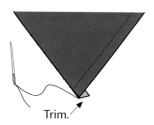

Trim.

9. To end your stitching, take the needle to the wrong side of the fabric, knot off, and insert the needle between the fabric layers. Bring the needle out about $1/2$" away and trim the thread next to the fabric. The thread tail will be hidden inside the fabric layers. **Optional:** Some quilters trim away the background fabric behind the shapes. This is personal preference, but it's not strictly necessary. If you trim, leave at least a $1/4$" seam allowance all around and be careful not to cut into the appliqué fabric.

10. Place the appliqué on a towel, wrong side up, or lay a towel over the appliqué and press on the wrong side so as not to flatten the appliqué. Spritz with water first or use a shot of steam from your iron.

TIPS FOR HAND APPLIQUÉ

- Place a pillow on your lap to support and stabilize your work while stitching.

- You can trim seam allowances as you stitch. This gives you a narrow seam allowance that is easy to turn under smoothly and eliminates frayed fabric edges. It also decreases bulk in small pieces.

- When stitching inner curves, clip into the seam allowance, just enough to allow the seam allowance to ease under smoothly.

- For tiny pieces, use a bit of fabric glue stick on the end of a toothpick to help hold seam allowances under.

QUILTING AND BINDING

When your quilt top is complete, press it carefully, making sure the seam allowances are flat and pressed in the correct direction. Prepare the backing so that it's at least 2" larger than the quilt top on all sides, and press it to remove any wrinkles. Place the backing wrong side up on a flat surface and use masking tape or binder clips to hold it in place. Layer it with your choice of batting and the quilt top. Smooth out any wrinkles and baste with thread for hand quilting or rustproof safety pins 3" to 4" apart for machine quilting.

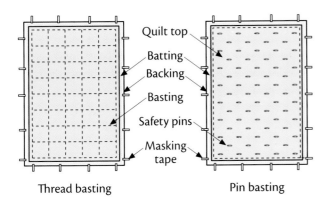

Thread basting   Pin basting

QUILTING

Quilt by hand or machine, as you prefer. Most of the quilts in this book were machine quilted, but I do like to hand quilt when time is not an issue.

After quilting, trim and square up the quilt top to prepare it for binding. I have a 20½" square Omnigrip ruler that comes in very handy for this. If there are blocks along the edge of the quilt, be sure to leave ¼" beyond block points when trimming.

BINDING

I rarely know what binding fabric I will use until I finish the quilting. I prefer to see the almost-completed quilt and then decide what it needs for the final touch. Sometimes I don't want the binding to stand out, so I'll look for a fabric print that blends with the overall quilt. Other times, a binding can serve as an accent color, act as a frame, or add a surprise element to the quilt.

For small quilts, I usually cut binding strips 2⅛" wide. This gives a narrow finished binding that easily covers the stitching when you turn it to the back and hand sew it to the backing. The binding yardage for these projects is calculated using 2¼"-wide strips, so you can cut a slightly wider or narrower binding if you prefer.

1. Cut the number of binding strips indicated in the project instructions. You need enough length to go around the quilt plus about 12" for joining seams and mitering corners. For most bindings, cut strips across the width of the fabric. For bias binding, cut strips on the bias, using the 45° line on your ruler as shown.

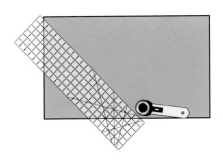

2. Sew the binding strips together into one long length using diagonal seams. For straight-grain strips, place strips together at right angles and stitch as shown. Trim the excess fabric. For bias strips, align the strips as shown and stitch. Press the seam allowances open.

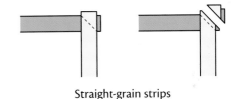

Straight-grain strips

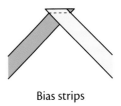

Bias strips

3. Fold the strip in half lengthwise, wrong sides together, and press.

4. If you want to add a hanging sleeve that is sewn into the binding, refer to "Hanging Sleeve" on page 13 and make it now. Pin or baste it to the top edge of the quilt.

5. Beginning on one side of the quilt, align the raw edges of the binding strip with the edge of the quilt. Using a ¼" seam allowance, start sewing about 6" from the cut end of the binding, leaving the tail unsewn. Use a walking foot if you have one to feed the layers through evenly. Stop sewing ¼" from the corner of the quilt and backstitch. Trim the threads.

CHECK THE CORNERS FIRST

Before sewing, lay out the binding all around the quilt to preview it. Make sure that a seam won't fall at any of the corners. Rearrange the binding if it does. A seam at the corner will make the mitered corner a bit bulky and harder to execute.

6. Position the quilt to sew along the next side. Fold the binding up to create a 45°-angle fold at the corner and a 90° angle with the top edge of the quilt. Fold the binding down to align the edges with the next side of the quilt. Begin sewing at the fold and continue to the next corner, stopping ¼" away. Repeat the folding and stitching process and continue around the quilt.

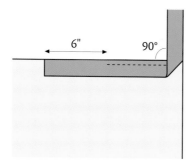

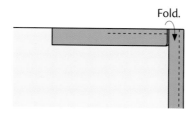

Fold.

7. When you are about 6" to 8" from the starting point, stop stitching and remove the quilt from the machine. Overlap the ending tail with the beginning tail. Trim the binding ends so that the overlap is equal to the binding width; for a 2⅛"-wide binding strip, the overlap should be 2⅛".

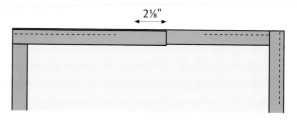

2⅛"

8. Open up the ends of the folded binding and pin them right sides together at right angles as shown. Mark a diagonal line from corner to corner and stitch on the drawn line.

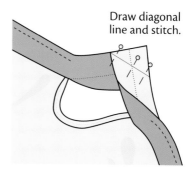

Draw diagonal line and stitch.

9. Trim the excess fabric, leaving a ¼" seam allowance. Press the seam allowance open (finger-pressing is fine) and refold the binding. Align it with the raw edges of the quilt and finish sewing it in place.

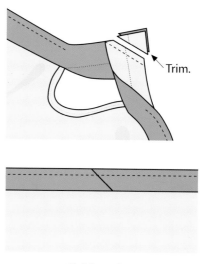

Trim.

Finish sewing.

10. Fold the binding over the edge of the quilt and hand sew it to the back of the quilt, covering the line of machine stitching. Fold the miters at each corner in the opposite direction of the miter on the front. I like to take three stitches in the folded miter on both the front and back to hold it in place and keep it nice and flat.

HANGING SLEEVE

For displaying your quilt on a wall, make a hanging sleeve so that you can slip a rod through it. Use leftover backing fabric or any coordinating or contrasting fabric that you like.

1. Cut a rectangle of fabric that is 6" to 8" wide and 1" shorter than the width of your quilt. Fold the short ends over ½" and then ½" again to create a hem. Machine stitch the hem in place. I often use one of the decorative stitches on my machine to hem the hanging sleeve. That's one of the few times I get to use them.

Hem the ends.

2. Fold the fabric in half wrong sides together and press. Pin or baste the sleeve in place along the top edge of the quilt. The raw edges will be enclosed in the binding.

Raw edges

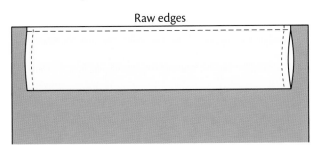

Baste to quilt.

3. After the binding is completed, move up the lower edge of the sleeve ¼" to ⅜" and pin it in place. This will provide extra room for the rod. Blindstitch the sleeve in place by hand along the bottom and side edges.

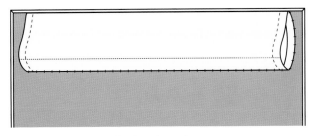

Blindstitch in place.

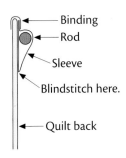

Binding
Rod
Sleeve
Blindstitch here.
Quilt back

ADD A LABEL

Add a label to the back of your quilt that includes your name, date, hometown, and state. Include any other information that is relevant, such as the name of the quilt or block, or, if the quilt is a gift, the name of the recipient and a special sentiment for the occasion. Be as creative as you like with fabric pens and markers, and then sew the label to the backing using a hand appliqué stitch.

Pinwheel PIROUETTE

Soft, sweet 1930's reproduction prints combined with hand-dyed solid fabrics make an easy and charming first project. The block is a typical Pinwheel, but it also goes by numerous related and unrelated names, including Windmill, Water Wheel, Watermill, Mosaic, and Crow's Foot, to list a few. Make it for a doll quilt or use it in the center of your table topped with a bouquet of daffodils. I washed and dried the finished quilt to give it a timeworn and well-loved look.

Quilt size: 19½" x 19½"   **Block size: 2¾" x 2¾"**

MATERIALS

½ yard of lavender '30s reproduction print for outer border and binding

1 fat quarter of yellow '30s reproduction print for blocks and setting pieces

1 fat quarter of green solid for 1 block and inner border

3" x 5" piece *each* of 8 solid fabrics in green, blues, pinks, lavender, and orange for blocks*

¾ yard of fabric for backing

24" x 24" piece of batting

Perfect for 5" x 5" charm squares!

CUTTING

From *each* of the 9 solid fabrics, cut:

* 2 squares, 2¼" x 2¼"; cut in half diagonally to make 4 triangles (36 total)

From the yellow print, cut:

* 18 squares, 2¼" x 2¼"; cut in half diagonally to make 36 triangles

* 4 squares, 3¼" x 3¼"

* 2 squares, 5¼" x 5¼"; cut into quarters diagonally to make 8 side triangles

* 2 squares, 3" x 3"; cut in half diagonally to make 4 corner triangles

From the remainder of the green solid, cut:

* 4 strips, 1¼" x 21"

From the lavender print, cut:

* 2 strips, 3½" x 42"

* 3 strips, 2⅛" x 42"

PIECING THE BLOCKS

1. Sew each solid 2¼" triangle to a yellow print 2¼" triangle to make a half-square-triangle unit. Press. Make a total of 36 units.

Make 36.

2. Arrange four matching half-square-triangle units as shown; sew into rows and press. Sew the rows together to make a Pinwheel block. Repeat to make a total of nine blocks.

Make 9.

ASSEMBLING THE QUILT

1. Arrange the blocks, yellow print 3¼" squares, and yellow print triangles in diagonal rows as shown in the quilt diagram. Sew the pieces together into rows and press. Sew the rows together; press. Add the corner triangles last; press.

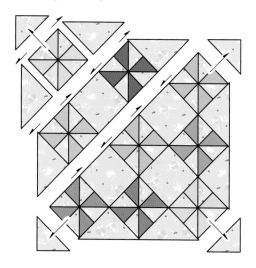

2. Trim to square up the quilt, making sure to leave ¼" beyond the points of the Pinwheel blocks.

3. Measure the width of the quilt top through the center and cut two green 1¼" x 21" inner-border strips to this length. Sew to the top and bottom of the quilt top; press. Measure the length of the quilt top through the center and cut the remaining two inner-border strips to this length. Sew them to the sides of the quilt and press. Measure and add the lavender print 3½"-wide outer-border strips in the same manner.

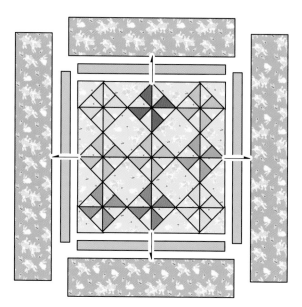

FINISHING

Layer, baste, quilt, and add the lavender print binding. Refer to "Quilting and Binding" on page 11 for details. I quilted in the ditch around the pinwheels and quilted a maple leaf in the alternate blocks using a paper-piecing foundation as a guide. The borders were quilted in the orange peel design.

Four-Patch PINWHEELS

This simple Pinwheel block doesn't even require any triangles. It's perfect for using up odds and ends of fabrics, even very small scraps. Choose two background prints that you really love—one for the blocks and one for the setting triangles and sashing. The rest can come from your scrap basket. I created this block when doodling one day and never did find an official name for it.

Quilt size: 31½" x 41½"   Block size: 6" x 6"

MATERIALS

1 yard of light print 1 for sashing and setting triangles

⅝ yard of light print 2 for block backgrounds

½ yard *total* of scraps of assorted medium to dark prints and solid fabrics for blocks and sashing squares

⅓ yard of light dotted print for binding

1½ yards of fabric for backing

36" x 46" piece of batting

CUTTING

From the assorted medium to dark prints and solid fabrics, cut a *total* of:

- 89 squares, 1½" x 1½"
- 72 rectangles, 1½" x 2½"

From light print 2, cut:

- 7 strips, 2½" x 42"; cut into 72 rectangles, 2½" x 3½"

From light print 1, cut:

- 9 strips, 1½" x 42"; cut into:
  - 36 rectangles, 1½" x 6½"
  - 10 rectangles, 1½" x 7½"
  - 2 rectangles, 1½" x 8½"
- 3 squares, 11½" x 11½"; cut into quarters diagonally to make 12 side triangles (2 are extra)
- 2 squares, 6¾" x 6¾"; cut in half diagonally to make 4 corner triangles

From the light dotted print, cut:

- 4 strips, 2⅛" x 42"

PIECING THE BLOCKS

1. Using the assorted medium or dark pieces, sew a 1½" square to each 1½" x 2½" rectangle. Press. Make 72.

Make 72.

2. Sew each unit from step 1 to a 2½" x 3½" light print 2 rectangle. Press. Make 72.

Make 72.

3. Sew four units from step 2 together to make a block. Press. Repeat to make a total of 18 blocks.

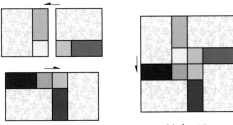

Make 18.

ASSEMBLING THE QUILT

1. Arrange the blocks, light print 1 sashing strips, medium or dark sashing squares, and light print 1 setting triangles in diagonal rows as shown in the quilt diagram. Sew together into rows and press.

2. Sew the rows together; press. Add the corner triangles last; press.

3. Trim and square up the quilt as needed, making sure to leave ¼" beyond the points of the sashing strips.

FINISHING

Layer, baste, quilt, and add the dotted print binding. Refer to "Quilting and Binding" on page 11 for details. I quilted a spiral in each block, partial spirals in the setting triangles, and a random wavy line in the sashing.

1½" x 6½"
1½" x 8½"
1½" x 7½"
1½" x 6½"
1½" x 7½"
1½" x 8½"

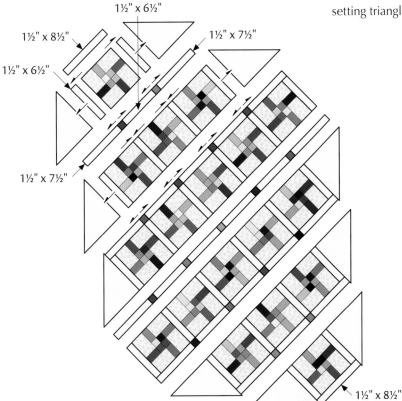

Pinwheel CHARM

I have been collecting hand-dyed solid fabrics for years and just love their soft look and wonderful colors. In this quilt, I combined them with a cheery Japanese floral print in a simple block design. The block apparently has not been assigned a name in historical quilt literature, but quilt historian Barbara Brackman has called it Charm. It's really just a square divided into two equal, odd-shaped, four-sided patches, which creates a tessellated pattern that's lots of fun to piece.

Quilt size: 26½" x 26½"   Block size: 4" x 4"

MATERIALS

¾ yard of dark print for blocks and inner and outer borders

⅜ yard *total* of assorted solid fabrics for blocks*

¼ yard of light solid fabric for middle border

¼ yard of dark print for binding

1 yard of fabric for backing

31" x 31" piece of batting

Perfect for 5" x 5" charm squares! You'll need 25; one charm square is enough for one block.

CUTTING

From the dark print, cut:

- 4 strips, 2½" x 42"
- 2 strips, 1½" x 20½"
- 2 strips, 1½" x 22½"
- 2 strips, 1½" x 24½"
- 2 strips, 1½" x 25½"

From the assorted solid fabrics, cut a *total* of:

- 25 strips, 2½" x 7"*

From the light solid fabric, cut:

- 2 strips, 1½" x 22½"
- 2 strips, 1½" x 25½"

From the dark print for binding, cut:

- 3 strips, 2⅛" x 42"

If you are using charm squares, cut each charm square in half to make 2 strips, 2½" x 5.

CUTTING AND PIECING THE BLOCKS

1. Prepare a paper cutting guide using the pattern on page 23. I used graph paper, but any paper will work. Include the stitching lines to help maintain accuracy when cutting.

2. Layer two dark print 2½" x 42" strips together, right sides up, and press. Trim and square up one end of the layered strips.

3. Place the paper guide on the strips, aligning it with the cut edges of the strips as shown. Place a ruler over the paper, positioning the ¼" line of the ruler on the stitching line, and cut with a rotary cutter. Rotate the cutting guide and make a cut along the straight edge. You should be able to cut about 25 patches from each 42" strip. Prepare the two remaining dark print 2½" x 42" strips as in step 2, and continue cutting until you have cut a total of 100 pieces.

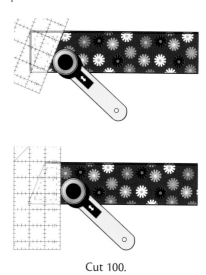

Cut 100.

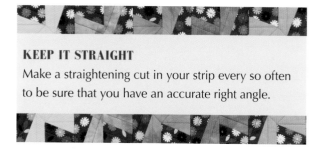

KEEP IT STRAIGHT
Make a straightening cut in your strip every so often to be sure that you have an accurate right angle.

4. Layer the solid strips in pairs and cut four matching pieces for each block, for a total of 100.

5. Place the narrow end of each solid piece right sides together with the wide end of a print piece, offsetting the points by ¼". Sew and press. Make four matching units for each block.

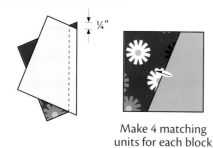

Make 4 matching units for each block (100 total).

6. Arrange four matching units as shown and sew into rows. Press. Sew the rows together to make the block. Repeat to make a total of 25 blocks.

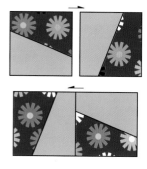
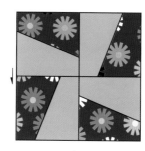

Make 25.

ASSEMBLING THE QUILT

1. Arrange the blocks in five rows of five blocks each, rotating the blocks as needed so that the seams will butt together. Sew into rows and press. Sew the rows together; press.

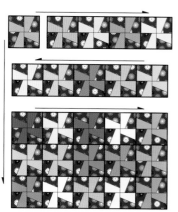

2. Sew the dark print 1½" x 20½" strips to the sides of the quilt. Press. Sew the dark print 1½" x 22½" strips to the top and bottom. Press. Add the light solid 1½" x 22½" strips to the top and bottom.

3. Sew the light solid 1½" x 25½" strips to the dark print 1½" x 25½" strips. Press.

4. Add the border units from step 3 and the dark print 1½" x 24½" strips to the quilt, using a partial seam to begin. Start in the center of the top edge of the quilt, sewing the dark print strip to the quilt as shown in the quilt diagram. Work counterclockwise around the quilt to add the borders, finishing the top seam last (see illustration below). Press all seam allowances outward.

FINISHING

Layer, baste, quilt, and add the binding. Refer to "Quilting and Binding" on page 11 for details. I quilted in the ditch of the blocks and borders and added two different straight line designs in the solid patches.

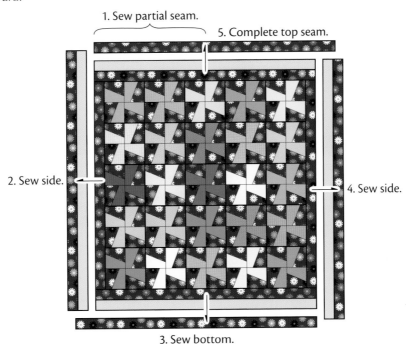

1. Sew partial seam.

5. Complete top seam.

2. Sew side.

4. Sew side.

3. Sew bottom.

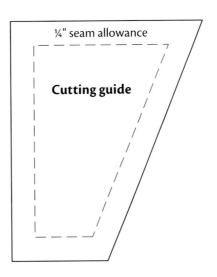

¼" seam allowance

Cutting guide

Nothing but PINWHEELS

I find this Pinwheel block, also known as Electric Fan, interesting because it creates secondary pinwheels at the block intersections. Choose two colors for the blocks for two different-colored pinwheels as I did, or make the central pinwheels different colors and the secondary pinwheels a consistent color. Either way, the central pinwheels will be of one fabric, and the secondary pinwheels will have four different fabrics. Fun! Antique quilts often don't include borders, because larger pieces of fabric weren't always available. I wanted this quilt to look old-fashioned, so I adopted that borderless strategy and used "nothing but pinwheels."

Quilt size: 25½" x 30½"   Block size: 5" x 5"

MATERIALS

¾ yard of light print for blocks

½ yard *total* of assorted brown prints for blocks*

½ yard *total* of assorted pink prints for blocks*

¼ yard of brown-and-pink print for binding

1 yard of fabric for backing

30" x 35" piece of batting

Perfect for 5" x 5" charm squares! You'll need 30 each of pink prints and brown prints.

CUTTING

From the light print, cut:

- 6 strips, 3¾" x 42"; crosscut into 60 squares, 3¾" x 3¾". Cut each square into quarters diagonally to make 240 triangles.

From the assorted brown prints, cut a *total* of:

- 30 squares, 3¾" x 3¾"; cut into quarters diagonally to make 120 triangles

From the assorted pink prints, cut:

- 30 squares, 3¾" x 3¾"; cut into quarters diagonally to make 120 triangles

From the brown-and-pink print, cut:

- 3 strips, 2⅛" x 42"

PIECING THE BLOCKS

For each block, select eight light print triangles, four matching brown print triangles, and four matching pink print triangles.

1. Sew a brown print triangle to a light print triangle along the short side as shown. Press. Make four. Repeat with the four pink print triangles. For this block, always sew with either the brown or the pink triangle on top and the light print on the bottom.

Make 4 of each.

2. Sew a pink unit to a brown unit. Make four quarter-square-triangle units. Press the seam allowances of two units toward the brown triangles and two units toward the pink triangles.

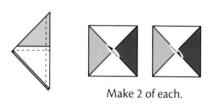

Make 2 of each.

GOING UP OR DOWN?

If you're using a directional print for the pink or brown triangles, arrange the units as you would like them to appear in the block *before* you press.

3. Arrange the units as shown. Sew together in rows and press the seam allowances of both rows toward the brown. Sew the rows together and press.

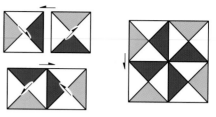

4. Repeat steps 1–3 to make a total of 30 blocks.

ASSEMBLING AND FINISHING THE QUILT

1. Arrange the blocks in six rows of five blocks each. Sew the blocks into rows and press. Sew the rows together; press.

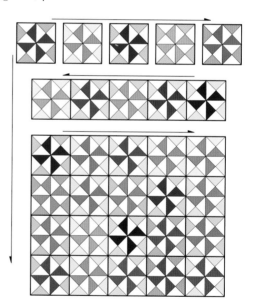

2. Layer, baste, quilt, and add the brown-and-pink print binding. Refer to "Quilting and Binding" on page 11 for details. I quilted an overall clamshell motif, which adds some curves to the design and enhances the quilt's old-fashioned look.

Twice As NICE

I always like quilt designs that create a diagonal pattern, and using these two different blocks gives the impression of an on-point setting. The central blocks are called Turnstile, and the blocks that surround them are a variation of The Spinner. Everything in this quilt is scrappy— take advantage of it and use up some odds and ends. Then you can purchase more fabric, guilt-free!

Quilt size: 40½" x 40½"   Block size: 5" x 5"
Half Block size: 2½" x 5"   Quarter Block size: 2½" x 2½"

MATERIALS

2⅛ yards *total* of assorted light prints for blocks and border

1 yard *total* of assorted medium to dark prints for blocks

⅜ yard of medium print for binding

2½ yards of fabric for backing

45" x 45" piece of batting

CUTTING

As you cut, keep the pieces for each block together to make piecing easier.

FOR ONE TURNSTILE BLOCK (Cut 24 total.)

From 1 light print, cut:

- 2 squares, 3⅜" x 3⅜"; cut in half diagonally to make 4 triangles

- 1 square, 3¾" x 3¾"; cut into quarters diagonally to make 4 triangles

From 1 medium or dark print, cut:

- 1 square, 3¾" x 3¾"; cut into quarters diagonally to make 4 triangles

FOR ONE SPINNER BLOCK (Cut 25 total.)

From 1 light print, cut:

- 2 squares, 3⅜" x 3⅜"; cut in half diagonally to make 4 triangles

- 4 squares, 1¾" x 1¾"

From 1 medium or dark print, cut:

- 4 squares, 2⅛" x 2⅛"; cut in half diagonally to make 8 triangles

FOR ONE HALF-SPINNER BLOCK (Cut 12 total.)

From 1 light print, cut:

- 1 square, 3⅜" x 3⅜"; cut in half diagonally to make 2 triangles

- 2 squares, 1¾" x 1¾"

From 1 medium or dark print, cut:

- 2 squares, 2⅛" x 2⅛"; cut in half diagonally to make 4 triangles

FOR TWO QUARTER-SPINNER BLOCKS (Cut 4 total.)

From 1 light print, cut:

- 1 square, 3⅜" x 3⅜"; cut in half diagonally to make 2 triangles

- 2 squares, 1¾" x 1¾"

From *each of 2* different medium or dark prints, cut:

- 1 square, 2⅛" x 2⅛"; cut in half diagonally to make 2 triangles (4 total)

FOR BORDER AND BINDING

From the assorted light prints, cut a *total* of:

- 16 rectangles, 2½" x 5½"

From the medium print for binding, cut:

- 5 strips, 2⅛" x 42"

PIECING THE TURNSTILE BLOCKS

1. Using the pieces cut for one block, sew each of the four medium or dark 3¾" triangles to a light print 3¾" triangle. Press.

Make 4.

2. Sew each unit from step 1 to a light print 3⅜" triangle. Press.

Make 4.

3. Arrange and sew the units from step 2 together as shown to make the block.

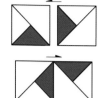

4. Repeat steps 1–3 to make a total of 24 blocks.

PIECING THE SPINNER BLOCKS

1. Using the pieces cut for one block, sew two medium or dark 2⅛" triangles to adjacent sides of a light print 1¾" square as shown. Press seam allowances toward the triangles. Repeat to make a total of four units.

Make 4.

2. Sew a unit from step 1 to each of the four light print 3⅜" triangles. Press.

Make 4.

3. Arrange and sew the units from step 2 together as shown to make the block. Press.

4. Repeat steps 1–3 to make a total of 25 blocks.

5. To make the Half-Spinner blocks, repeat steps 1 and 2 to make two units using the pieces you cut for one block. Arrange and sew the units together as shown to make the half block. Repeat to make a total of 12 blocks.

Make 12.

6. To make the Quarter-Spinner blocks, repeat steps 1 and 2 using the pieces you cut for one block. Repeat to make a total of four blocks.

Make 4.

COLOR OPTIONS

Here are some ideas to give this quilt a different look.

Use just one color for the medium and dark fabrics for a classic look, such as red or blue with the cream. Or choose two favorite colors, using one for the Turnstile blocks and one for the Spinner blocks. To make a holiday quilt, use only red and green fabrics for the medium and dark fabrics, keeping the background light.

Or, try this: Substitute dark for light fabrics and light for the medium and dark fabrics. I think it would be interesting to use all dark or medium blue fabrics for the background, and then use pale yellow prints for the Turnstile blocks and cream or white prints for the Spinner blocks. Blue, white, and yellow is always an appealing combination. Or use red for the Turnstile blocks and white prints for the Spinner blocks if you prefer a red, white, and blue version.

ASSEMBLING AND FINISHING THE QUILT

1. Arrange the blocks on a design wall, alternating them as shown in the quilt diagram. Add the half blocks and 2½" x 5½" rectangles along the outer edges. Add a quarter block in each corner. Sew the blocks into rows and press. Sew the rows together; press.

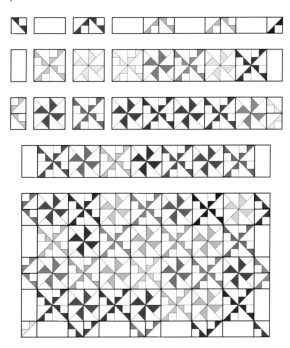

2. Layer, baste, quilt, and add the medium print binding. Refer to "Quilting and Binding" on page 11 for details. I didn't want the quilting to detract from the piecing, so I kept the quilting simple and stitched in the ditch horizontally, vertically, and diagonally.

Windmill ROW

Vertical strip settings are the perfect showcase for any gorgeous fabric that you want to feature without cutting it into small pieces. You can really appreciate the fabric this way. I used the two large-scale prints as a foundation for choosing colors and prints for the blocks. This block design is called Windmill and it has the appearance of an on-point block, but without the need for setting triangles. I'd also like to try the blocks set together without the vertical sashing strips: you'd get small four-patch units at the block intersections. So many blocks, so little time!

Quilt size: 40½" x 46½"   Block size: 6" x 6"

MATERIALS

1⅓ yards of gold print for outer border and binding

⅔ yard *total* of assorted light prints for blocks

½ yard *total* of assorted medium prints for blocks

⅜ yard of blue print for wide vertical sashing

⅓ yard *total* of assorted medium-dark or dark prints for blocks

⅓ yard of gray striped fabric for narrow vertical sashing and inner border

2½ yards of fabric for backing

45" x 51" piece of batting

CUTTING

FOR ONE BLOCK (Cut 18 total.)

From 1 light print, cut:

- 1 square, 4¼" x 4¼"; cut into quarters diagonally to make 4 triangles

- 4 squares, 2" x 2"

From 1 medium print, cut:

- 4 squares, 2⅜" x 2⅜"; cut in half diagonally to make 8 triangles

From 1 medium-dark or dark print, cut:

- 1 square, 4¼" x 4¼"; cut into quarters diagonally to make 4 triangles

FOR SASHING STRIPS, BORDERS, AND BINDING

From the blue print, cut:

- 2 strips, 5½" x 36½"

From the gray striped fabric, cut:

- 6 strips, 1" x 36½"

- 2 strips, 1" x 40½"

From the gold print, cut on the *lengthwise* grain:

- 2 strips, 5" x 36½"

- 2 strips, 5" x 40½"

- 5 strips, 2⅛" x 42"

PIECING THE BLOCKS

1. Using the pieces cut for one block, sew two medium print 2⅜" triangles to adjacent sides of each light print 2" square. Press the seam allowances as shown.

Make 2. Make 1. Make 1.

2. Sew a dark 4¼" triangle to each light print 4¼" triangle along the short edges. Press. Make four units.

Make 4.

3. Sew the units from steps 1 and 2 together. Press the seam allowances as shown, paying careful attention to the direction in which the units from step 1 were pressed.

4. Arrange the units from step 3 so that the pressed seams are positioned as shown. Sew the four units together to make the Windmill block.

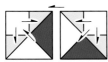  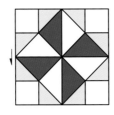

5. Repeat steps 1–4 to make a total of 18 blocks.

ASSEMBLING THE QUILT

1. Refer to the assembly diagram below to arrange the blocks in three vertical rows of six blocks each. Position the blocks so that the center seam allowance is pressed toward the bottom of the block and the seams in each block butt together nicely. Sew the blocks into rows. Press the seam allowances toward the bottom of the row.

2. Position the block rows, gray striped 1" x 36½" strips, blue print 5½" x 36½" strips, and gold print 5" x 36½" strips as shown in the quilt diagram; sew together to make the quilt center. Press.

3. Sew a gray striped 1" x 40½" strip to each gold print 5" x 40½" strip. Press. Sew to the top and bottom of the quilt. Press.

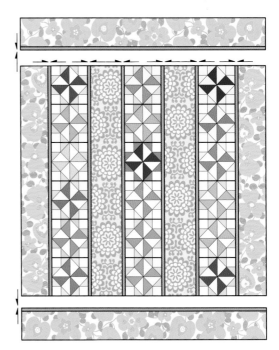

FINISHING

Layer, baste, quilt, and add the binding. Refer to "Quilting and Binding" on page 11 for details. I quilted in the ditch of vertical and horizontal seams first, and then I quilted continuous curves in the blocks and followed the print in the strips and borders.

Three of HEARTS

The combination of red and white is one of those classic color schemes that never goes out of style. Here I combined appliquéd hearts and traditional Pinwheel blocks in many shades of red on a white-and-red print background fabric. Pinwheels dance around the hearts, creating a good pairing as well. Make this quilt to cheer up a blank wall, use on a table for Valentine's Day, or as a gift to brighten someone's day.

Quilt size: 26" x 28"   Block size: 3" x 3"

MATERIALS

1 yard of cream print for background and borders

⅜ yard *total* of assorted red prints for hearts and blocks

⅛ yard or 1 fat quarter *each of 2* different red prints for sashing

¼ yard of red print for binding*

1 yard of fabric for backing

30" x 32" piece of batting

Or make a scrappy binding with ¼ yard total of assorted red prints.

CUTTING

From the cream print, cut:

- 1 rectangle, 7½" x 18"

- 2 strips, 2⅜" x 42"; crosscut into 32 squares, 2⅜" x 2⅜". Cut each square in half diagonally to make 64 triangles.

- 1 strip, 5½" x 42"; crosscut into 6 squares, 5½" x 5½". Cut each square into quarters diagonally to make 24 side triangles.

- 1 strip, 3" x 42"; crosscut into 8 squares, 3" x 3". Cut each square in half diagonally to make 16 corner triangles.

- 1 strip, 4¾" x 42"; crosscut into 2 strips, 4¾" x 17½"

- 1 strip, 5¾" x 20"; crosscut into 2 rectangles, 5¾" x 9"

From the assorted red prints, cut a *total* of:

- 32 squares, 2⅜" x 2⅜"; cut in half diagonally to make 64 triangles

From *each* of the 2 red prints for sashing, cut:

- 2 strips, 1½" x 17½" (4 total)

From the red print for binding, cut:

- 3 strips, 2⅛" x 42" (or strips to total 120")

APPLIQUÉING THE HEARTS

1. Referring to "Hand Appliqué" on page 8 and the pattern on page 37, prepare the heart appliqués.

2. Fold the cream print 7½" x 18" rectangle in half both ways to mark the vertical and horizontal centers. Position and pin the three hearts in place on the rectangle so that they are centered and spaced evenly. The background is cut slightly oversized so that you can trim it to size after stitching the appliqués.

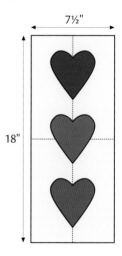

3. Appliqué the hearts in place.

PIECING THE PINWHEEL BLOCKS

1. Sew each red print 2⅜" triangle to a cream 2⅜" triangle along the long edges. Press. Make 64 half-square-triangle units.

Make 64.

2. Sew two different units from step 1 together (you'll need two matching pairs for each block), and then sew matching pairs together to make the Pinwheel block. Arrange the units to make eight blocks with triangles spinning one way, and eight blocks spinning the opposite direction.

Make 8 of each.

ASSEMBLING THE QUILT

1. Trim the appliquéd center rectangle so that it measures 7" x 17½". Be sure to keep the hearts centered.

2. Sew a red print 1½" x 17½" strip to each side of the appliquéd center. Press.

3. Arrange four Pinwheel blocks (spinning in the same direction) with six side triangles and four corner triangles as shown. Sew together into diagonal units, pressing the seam allowances as indicated. Sew the units together to make a Pinwheel row. Make four Pinwheel rows.

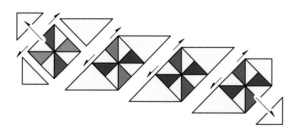

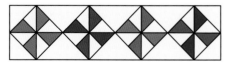

Make 2.

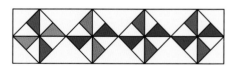

Make 2.

4. Sew matching Pinwheel rows to each side of the quilt center. Press toward the red print strips.

5. Sew a cream print 4¾" x 17½" strip to each side of the quilt center. Press.

6. Sew a red print 1½" x 17½" strip to each of the remaining two Pinwheel rows. Press. Sew a cream print 5¾" x 9" rectangle to the right end of each row unit as shown. Press.

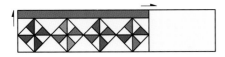

Make 2.

7. Sew the units from step 6 to the top and bottom of the quilt center. Press.

FINISHING

Layer, baste, quilt, and add the red print binding. Refer to "Quilting and Binding" on page 11 for details. I quilted a meandering leaf and vine in the background of the hearts and feathers in the outer borders.

Heart
Cut 3 from assorted red prints.

Pattern does not include seam allowance.

Hanging OUT

I love to hang laundry outside to dry on a breezy, sunny day. I find it to be one of those Zen-like activities that is very peaceful. I enjoy the sound wooden clothespins make as they are being pushed onto the clothesline rope, and it's very satisfying to see clean laundry hanging in a neat row and blowing in the wind. (Yes, I was one of those moms who used cloth diapers and hung them out to bleach in the sun.) The block that dances around these dresses is called Criss Cross.

Quilt size: 28½" x 24½"   Block size: 4" x 4"

MATERIALS

½ yard *total* of assorted light prints for blocks

½ yard *total* of assorted medium prints for blocks and appliqués

¼ yard *total* of assorted medium-dark or contrasting prints for blocks

¼ yard of orange print for inner border

1 fat quarter of white-and-yellow print for background

¼ yard of striped fabric for binding

1 yard of fabric for backing

29" x 33" piece of batting

Off-white pearl cotton for clothesline

Light tan embroidery floss or pearl cotton for clothespins

Fabric glue

CUTTING

FOR ONE BLOCK (Cut 22 total.)

From 1 light print, cut:

- 1 square, 4" x 4"; cut into quarters diagonally to make 4 triangles

From 1 medium print, cut:

- 4 rectangles, 1⅜" x 2½"

From 1 medium-dark or contrasting print, cut:

- 1 square, 2½" x 2½"; cut into quarters diagonally to make 4 triangles

FOR THE QUILT CENTER AND BINDING

From the white-and-yellow print, cut:

- 1 rectangle, 15" x 20"

From the orange print, cut:

- 2 strips, 1½" x 13½"

- 2 strips, 2" x 20½"

From the striped fabric, cut:

- 3 strips, 2⅛" x 42"

PIECING THE BLOCKS

1. Using the pieces cut for one block, sew a medium-dark or contrasting print triangle to each medium print rectangle as shown. Make four units; trim and press.

Trim.   Make 4.

2. Sew a light print triangle to each unit from step 1. Press.

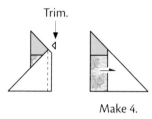

Trim.

Make 4.

3. Place two units from step 2 right sides together so that the rectangles are perpendicular to each other. Sew and press. Make two units and sew them together to complete the block. Trim and press.

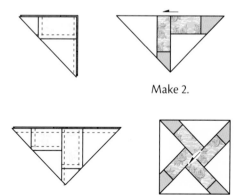

Make 2.

4. Repeat steps 1–3 to make a total of 22 blocks.

APPLIQUÉING THE CENTER

1. Referring to "Hand Appliqué" on page 8 and the patterns on pages 41–43, prepare the dress appliqués.

2. Appliqué the dresses to the white-and-yellow rectangle, using the diagram as a guide for

placement. The background is cut slightly oversized so that you can trim it to size after stitching the appliqués.

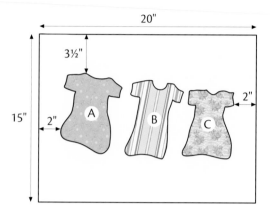

3. Trim the background to 13½" x 18½".

4. Position the pearl cotton on the background as desired for your clothesline. Using a toothpick, I placed tiny dots of fabric glue along the background to hold the "rope" in place for easy sewing. Allow to dry, and then stitch by hand using an overcast stitch.

5. Use the tan embroidery floss or pearl cotton to hand stitch the clothespins. Use a satin stitch for the clothespin body and add a French knot at the top if desired. Each clothespin should be approximately 1/16" x 1/4".

ACCESSORIZE!
Add rickrack or buttons to the dresses for embellishments.

ASSEMBLING THE QUILT

1. Sew the orange print 1½" x 13½" strips to the sides of the quilt. Press. Sew the orange print 2" x 20½" strips to the top and bottom. Press.

2. Arrange the Criss Cross blocks around the quilt. Sew four blocks together for each side border and seven blocks together for the top and bottom borders. Press.

3. Sew the side borders to the sides of the quilt. Press. Sew the top and bottom borders to the top and bottom. Press.

FINISHING

Layer, baste, quilt, and add the striped binding. Refer to "Quilting and Binding" on page 11 for details. I quilted a random, free-motion flower chain around the dresses and free-motion loops in the block backgrounds.

C
Cut 1 from assorted medium print.

Pattern does not include seam allowance.

Pattern does not include
seam allowance.

A
Cut 1 from assorted medium print.

Pattern does not include
seam allowance.

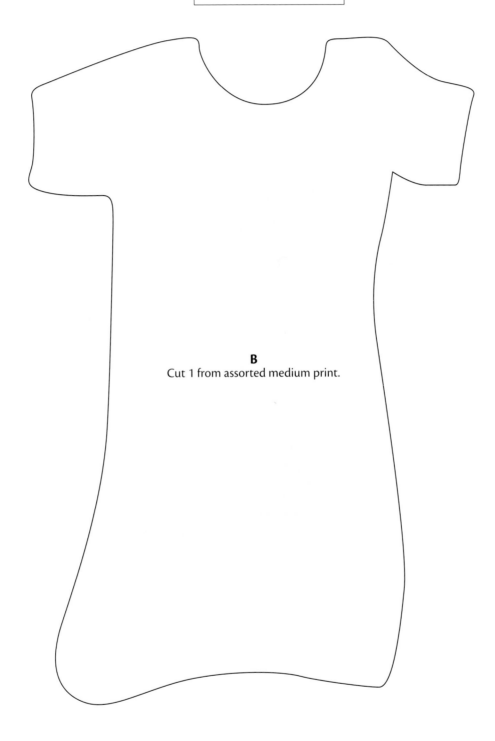

B
Cut 1 from assorted medium print.

Oklahoma MEMORIES

When I was growing up in northeastern Ohio, our family vacations were always spent in Oklahoma visiting my mother's family. My grandparents lived on a farm and raised wheat, sheep, cows, and chickens. The soil there is brick red and always made a huge impression on my brother and me. I remember bringing a jar of "red dirt" back to Ohio for show-and-tell. One of my favorite chores while visiting was gathering the eggs that the chickens laid in special hiding places all over the farm. The block I used for the windmill is called Pinwheel or Flying Kite.

Quilt size: 25" x 24½"   Block size: 5" x 5"

MATERIALS

½ yard *total* of assorted light checked, striped, and print fabrics for background

¼ yard *each* of 2 medium prints for top and right borders

1 fat eighth of medium print for left border

1 fat eighth of red-and-orange striped fabric for background

1 fat eighth of light print for Pinwheel block background

1 fat eighth of gray striped or print fabric for windmill legs

6" x 6" square *each* of 2 white prints and 1 yellow print for yo-yos

6" x 6" square of gold print for Pinwheel block

5" x 5" square of red print for Pinwheel block

Assorted scraps for chicken appliqués

¼ yard of fabric for binding

1 yard of fabric for backing

30" x 29" piece of batting

CUTTING

From the fat eighth of light print for Pinwheel block background, cut:

- 1 square, 3¾" x 3¾"; cut into quarters diagonally to make 4 triangles
- 1 strip, 1¼" x 16"

From the red print square, cut:

- 1 square, 3¾" x 3¾"; cut into quarters diagonally to make 4 triangles

From the gold print square, cut:

- 2 squares, 2⅝" x 2⅝"; cut in half diagonally to make 4 triangles

From the assorted light checked, striped, and print fabrics, cut:

- 1 rectangle, 2½" x 5½"
- 1 rectangle, 3" x 7½"
- 1 rectangle, 3" x 8"
- 1 rectangle, 3½" x 10"
- 1 rectangle, 3" x 11"
- 1 rectangle, 3½" x 12½"
- 1 rectangle, 5½" x 14"
- 1 rectangle, 5" x 17½"

From the red-and-orange striped fabric, cut:

- 1 rectangle, 4¼" x 18½"

From the gray striped fabric, cut:

- 2 strips, ¾" x 14"
- 1 rectangle, ¾" x 1½"
- 1 rectangle, ¾" x 2¾"
- 1 rectangle, 1" x 1½"

From the medium print for left border, cut:

- 1 strip, 4½" x 21"

From 1 medium print for top border, cut:

- 1 strip, 4" x 22"

From 1 medium print for right border, cut:

- 1 strip, 3½" x 24½"

From the binding fabric, cut:

- 3 strips, 2⅛" x 42"

PIECING THE WINDMILL BLOCK

1. Sew a red print 3¾" triangle to a light print 3¾" triangle along the short edges. Press. Repeat to make a total of four units.

Make 4.

2. Sew the gold print triangles to the 1¼" x 16" strip as shown, leaving about 1¼" above each triangle point. Press.

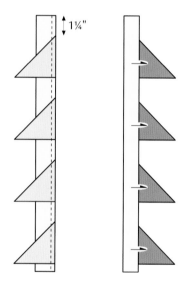

3. Cut the triangle units apart as shown, first cutting the right angle and then cutting the angled corner.

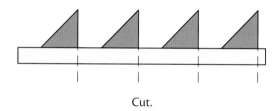

Cut.

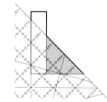

Make 4.

4. Sew the units from step 3 to the units from step 1. Press.

Make 4.

5. Arrange the units as shown and sew together to make the block. Press.

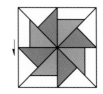

ASSEMBLING THE BACKGROUND

1. Sew the light print 2½" x 5½" rectangle to the bottom of the Pinwheel block. Press. Sew the 3" x 7½" rectangle to the right side as shown. Press.

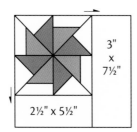

2. Continue adding rectangles as shown, ending with the red-and-orange rectangle to complete the background.

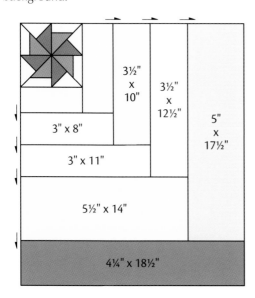

ADDING THE APPLIQUÉS

1. Referring to "Hand Appliqué" on page 8 and the patterns on pages 49 and 50, prepare the chicken appliqués. Feel free to use your favorite method of appliqué, but if you use the fusible-appliqué technique, be sure to reverse the patterns first.

2. Appliqué the chickens in place using the guide for placement, or let the chickens wander where you prefer. The background is cut slightly oversized so that you can trim it to size after stitching the appliqués. If you use a white print or polka-dot fabric for your chickens, you may want to trim the background fabric behind it so that it doesn't show through. (See page 10, step 9 of "Hand Appliqué.")

3. Appliqué the legs and supports of the windmill. Use a ruler and pencil to lightly draw two angled placement lines for the legs, beginning the lines ¼" to the left and right of the point at the bottom of the Pinwheel block and ending about one-third of the way into the red-and-orange rectangle. Refer to the quilt photo as needed. Align the long edge of one gray striped ¾" x 14" strip along the right line,

wrong side up, with the excess to the left of the line. Trim to the desired length, leaving enough to turn under and finish at the bottom edge. Machine stitch ¼" from the right edge of the strip.

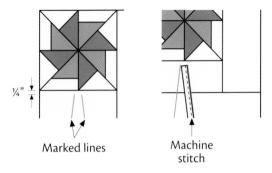

Marked lines   Machine
                                stitch

EASY MARKING

I used a Hera marker instead of a pencil to mark the straight lines for the windmill legs. This white plastic tool is available in quilt shops and art supply stores. It makes a visible crease in the fabric with no marks to worry about. I also used it to mark the diagonal lines for hand quilting.

4. Trim the seam allowance (to the right of the stitching) to ⅛" or less. Turn the strip to the right side and appliqué the other long raw edge and bottom by hand (or by machine if you prefer). Repeat for the other leg, placing the excess to the right of the marked line and stitching ¼" from the left edge of the strip. Use the gray striped ¾" x 1½" and ¾" x 2¾" rectangles to add the crosspieces in the same manner. Appliqué the top section last, using the 1" x 1½" rectangle.

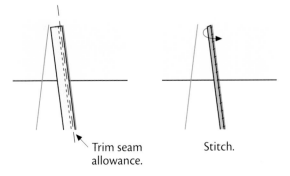

Trim seam   Stitch.
allowance.

5. Make one of each circle template using the three patterns on pages 50 and 51. Trace around each one onto the right side of the white print and yellow print squares. Cut ¼" outside the drawn line. I used the largest circle for the sun and the smaller ones for clouds.

6. Thread a needle and knot one end of the thread. Fold the seam allowance to the wrong side along the drawn line and sew a running stitch around the circle. Make sure the drawn line is folded over and included in the seam allowance. Take stitches ¼" to ⅜" long. Draw up the thread to gather the fabric and create the yo-yo. Take a few anchoring stitches in the center and knot off. Flatten the yo-yo and press lightly.

7. Appliqué the yo-yos to the background to create the sun and two clouds.

ADDING THE BORDERS AND FINISHING

1. Trim the background to 18" x 21", cutting any excess from the right and bottom edges.

2. Add the medium print 4½" x 21" strip to the left side of the background piece. Press. Add the top border piece and then the right border, pressing seam allowances after each.

3. Layer, baste, quilt, and add the binding. Refer to "Quilting and Binding" on page 11 for details. I hand quilted in a simple diagonal grid.

Patterns do not include seam allowances.

A
Cut 1 from assorted scraps.

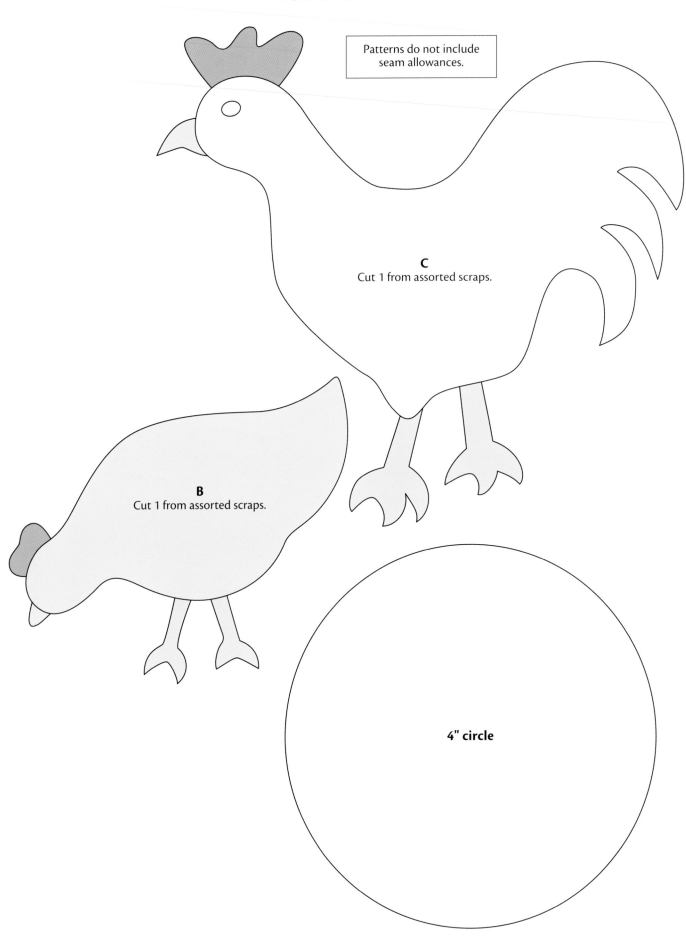

Patterns do not include
seam allowances.

C
Cut 1 from assorted scraps.

B
Cut 1 from assorted scraps.

4" circle

4½" circle

4⅞" circle

Xs and Os

This quilt started out as tic-tac-toe, but I couldn't stop at nine blocks. Batiks are such fabulous fabrics that it's easy to keep going. Here's your chance to show off some of the batiks in your own collection. The X block is a standard Pinwheel, but with the "corners cut off." I paired it with an O block just for fun.

Quilt size: 20" x 20"   **Block size: 4" x 4"**

MATERIALS

⅝ yard of light batik for blocks

4" x 6" piece *each* of 13 medium to dark batiks for X blocks

6" x 6" piece *each* of 12 medium batiks for O blocks

¼ yard of light plaid for binding*

¾ yard of fabric for backing

25" x 25" piece of batting

If you want to use a plaid cut on the bias, a fat quarter will yield longer bias strips for fewer seams.

CUTTING

From the light batik, cut:

- 2 strips, 2⅞" x 42"; crosscut into 26 squares, 2⅞" x 2⅞". Cut each square in half diagonally to make 52 triangles.
- 5 strips, 1⅝" x 42"; crosscut into 100 squares, 1⅝" x 1⅝"
- 1 strip, 1¾" x 42"; crosscut into 12 squares, 1¾" x 1¾"

From *each* 4" x 6" batik piece, cut:

- 2 squares, 2⅞" x 2⅞"; cut in half diagonally to make 4 triangles (52 total)

From *each* 6" x 6" batik piece, cut:

- 2 rectangles, 1¾" x 1⅞" (24 total)
- 2 rectangles, 1⅞" x 4½" (24 total)

From the light plaid, cut:

- 2⅛"-wide bias strips to total 94"

PIECING THE X BLOCKS

1. Sew a medium or dark batik 2⅞" triangle to a light batik 2⅞" triangle along the long edges to make a half-square-triangle unit. Press. Make four identical units.

Make 4.

2. Sew the four units together as shown to make a Pinwheel block.

3. Draw a line diagonally on the wrong side of each light batik 1⅝" square. Position a square on each corner of the Pinwheel block as shown and sew on the drawn lines. Trim the extra fabric to leave a ¼" seam allowance and press outward.

4. Repeat steps 1–3 to make a total of 13 X blocks.

PIECING THE O BLOCKS

1. Sew matching medium batik 1¾" x 1⅞" rectangles to opposite sides of a light batik 1¾" square. Press.

2. Sew matching medium batik 1⅞" x 4½" rectangles to the top and bottom of the unit from step 1. Press.

3. Position a marked light batik 1⅝" square on each corner of the block and sew on the drawn line. Trim the extra fabric to leave a ¼" seam allowance and press inward.

4. Repeat steps 1–3 to make a total of 12 O blocks.

ASSEMBLING AND FINISHING THE QUILT

1. Arrange the X and O blocks in five rows of five blocks each, alternating them as shown in the quilt diagram. Sew the blocks into rows and press. Sew the rows together; press.

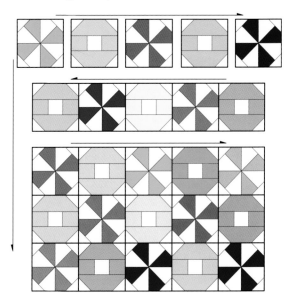

2. Layer, baste, quilt, and add the plaid binding. Refer to "Quilting and Binding" on page 11 for details. I quilted in the ditch so that the batiks would stand out without any distracting thread.

WhirlWIND

Japanese fabrics are another weakness of mine. Most, but not all, of the fabrics in this quilt are Japanese. I don't worry about mixing in another type of fabric. Sometimes the variety makes things more interesting. The block I used in this quilt has several names: Twin Sisters, Windmill, Water Wheel, Pinwheel, and Whirlwind.

Quilt size: 21" x 25½"   Block size: 3½" x 3½"

MATERIALS

14" x 14" piece *each* of 12 assorted prints for blocks and outer-border corner squares

¼ yard of purple floral for outer border

¼ yard of light taupe print for sashing and inner border

1 fat quarter of white print for blocks

2" x 18" piece of taupe print for sashing and inner-border squares

¼ yard of dark print for binding

⅞ yard of fabric for backing

26" x 31" piece of batting

Freezer paper OR half-square ruler

CUTTING

From *each* of the assorted prints, cut:

• 1 bias strip, 2" x 18"*

From the white print, cut:

• 6 bias strips, 1¾" x 18"*

From the light taupe print, cut:

• 4 strips, 1½" x 42"; crosscut into:
  • 17 rectangles, 1½" x 4"
  • 2 strips, 1½" x 13"
  • 2 strips, 1½" x 17½"

From the taupe print, cut:

• 10 squares, 1½" x 1½"

From the purple floral, cut:

• 2 strips, 3½" x 19½"
• 2 strips, 3½" x 15"

From 1 of the assorted prints, cut:

• 4 squares, 3½" x 3½"

From the dark print for binding, cut:

• 3 strips, 2⅛" x 42"

Cutting the strips on the bias will result in blocks with straight-grain edges.

PIECING THE BLOCKS

1. Sew an assorted-print bias strip to each long edge of a white bias strip. Press.

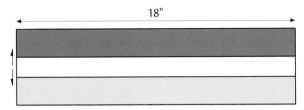

2. If you are using freezer paper, trace the cutting guide pattern on page 58 onto the dull side of a piece of freezer paper at least eight times; cut out the freezer-paper templates. Press eight templates, shiny side down, to the strip set from step 1 as shown, aligning the dashed line on the template with the appropriate seam. Cut out four along the bottom edge and four along the top edge. If you are using a half-square ruler, align the dashed yellow line at the top of the ruler with the upper seam line. Cut eight triangles from the strip set, four along the top and four along the bottom.

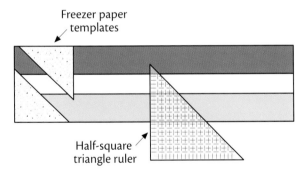

3. Gently remove the tiny triangle of the second fabric color from the point of each piece.

4. Sew each set of four matching units from step 2 together to make the blocks.

5. Repeat steps 1–4 to make a total of 12 blocks.

ASSEMBLING THE QUILT

1. Arrange the blocks in four horizontal rows of three blocks each, inserting the light taupe 1½" x 4" sashing strips between the blocks. Add the taupe sashing squares and sew the block rows and sashing rows as shown. Press. Sew the rows together and press.

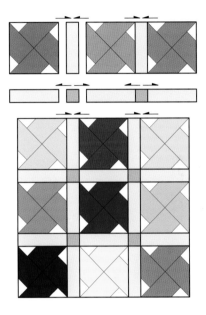

2. Add the light taupe 1½" x 17½" inner-border strips to the sides of the quilt. Press.

3. Sew a taupe 1½" corner square to each end of the light taupe 1½" x 13" inner-border strips. Press. Sew the strips to the top and bottom of the quilt.

4. Sew the purple floral 3½" x 19½" outer-border strips to the sides. Press.

5. Sew a 3½" corner square to each end of the purple floral 3½" x 15" outer-border strips. Press. Sew the strips to the top and bottom of the quilt.

FINISHING

Layer, baste, quilt, and add the dark print binding. Refer to "Quilting and Binding" on page 11 for details. I quilted in the ditch, quilted parallel lines in the sashing and border, and added crescent shapes inside the Pinwheel blocks.

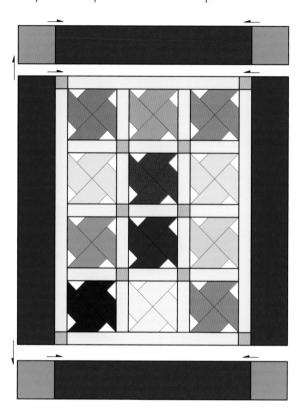

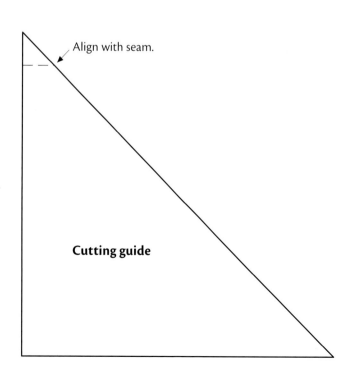

Align with seam.

Cutting guide

Wind FARM

When my husband showed me a photograph of wind turbines and jokingly suggested that I include them in my Pinwheel book, I couldn't resist the challenge. While I'm not a huge fan of paper-foundation piecing, it's great for unusual shapes and creating sharp, narrow points. It's the only way to go to make this Wind Turbine block.

Quilt size: 26½" x 31"   Block size: 6" x 6"

MATERIALS

1 fat eighth *each* or scraps of 9 assorted medium to dark blue prints for blocks

⅓ yard of dark blue print 1 for sashing and inner border

¼ yard of dark blue print 2 for side borders

⅛ yard of dark blue print 3 for top border

⅛ yard of dark blue print 4 for bottom border

⅛ yard *total* of assorted white prints for blocks

⅛ yard of light yellow print for blocks

⅓ yard of dark blue print 5 for binding

1 yard of fabric for backing

31" x 35" piece of batting

Foundation piecing material

CUTTING

From dark blue print 1, cut:

- 1 strip, 2½" x 42"; crosscut into 6 rectangles, 2½" x 6½"

- 2 rectangles, 3" x 6½"

- 1 rectangle, 2½" x 6½"

- 1 rectangle, 2" x 6½"

- 2 rectangles, 1½" x 6½"

- 2 strips, 1½" x 26"

From dark blue print 2, cut:

- 2 strips, 3½" x 26"

From dark blue print 3, cut:

- 1 strip, 3" x 26½"

From dark blue print 4, cut:

- 1 strip, 3" x 26½"

From dark blue print 5, cut:

- 4 strips, 2⅛" x 42"

PIECING THE BLOCKS

For each block, you'll need one medium or dark blue print and one white or light yellow print. I made three blocks with yellow blades and six with white.

1. Make nine copies each of foundation pattern sections A, B, and C on page 63, using a photocopier or tracing by hand. Use a lightweight paper or a product specifically made for foundation piecing.

2. For each section, begin with piece 1 and cut a piece of blue print bigger than you think you'll need. (I cut these pieces *a lot* bigger, and then I usually had enough.) For the blades (piece 2 in each section), cut three rectangles about 2¼" x 4".

3. Place the blue print for piece 1 right side up on the *wrong,* unmarked side of the foundation. Place a white or yellow piece right side down on the blue print, aligning it ¼" over the seam line between pieces 1 and 2. Hold everything up to a light to check that it's positioned correctly and that you'll have enough for a seam allowance.

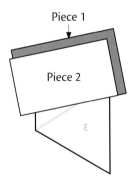

Piece 1

Piece 2

4. Insert a pin along the seam line and flip your fabric over to make sure you will have adequate coverage of the area for piece 2. When it's positioned correctly, pin to hold the pieces in place and turn the foundation over to the right side. Sew along the line, using a shortened stitch length (15 to 20 stitches per inch). Sew a few stitches outside the outer line; stop stitching at the point where the lines meet on the inside and backstitch.

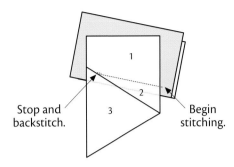

Stop and backstitch.   Begin stitching.

5. Remove the piece from the machine and trim the seam allowance to ¼". Press the seam, and then press piece 2 so that it covers the space.

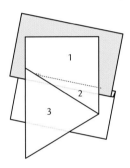

6. Continue adding pieces as needed in numerical order to complete each section. Place the finished sections on your cutting mat, foundation side up, and trim with a rotary cutter and ruler, leaving a ¼" seam allowance all around.

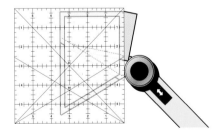

7. Sew sections A and B together, matching the seam lines, and press. Then join that unit to section C. Press. You can press the center seam allowances open to reduce bulk if desired.

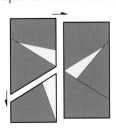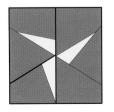

8. Repeat steps 2–7 to make a total of nine Wind Turbine blocks.

ASSEMBLING THE QUILT

1. Arrange the blocks in three rows of three blocks each. I rotated each block so that the blades would be going in random directions. The horizontal rows will be offset. Referring to the diagram, add the 6½"-long blue print 1 rectangles above and below each block and sew the blocks into vertical rows. Press the seam allowances toward the rectangles.

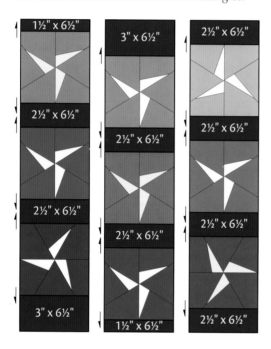

2. Sew the vertical rows together and press the seam allowances to the side.

3. Sew a 1½" x 26" blue print 1 strip to each side and press the seam allowances toward the strips.

4. Sew the 3½" x 26" blue print 2 strips to the sides of the quilt and press the seam allowances outward.

5. Sew the 3" x 26½" blue print 3 strip to the top of the quilt and the 3" x 26½" blue print 4 strip to the bottom. Press.

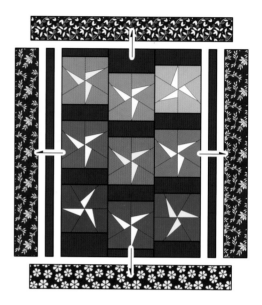

6. Carefully remove the foundation material from each block.

FINISHING

Layer, baste, quilt, and add the blue print 5 binding. Refer to "Quilting and Binding" on page 11 for details. I quilted around the pinwheels in a meandering design, adding parallel wavy lines in the sashing and random spiral designs in the borders.

Section A

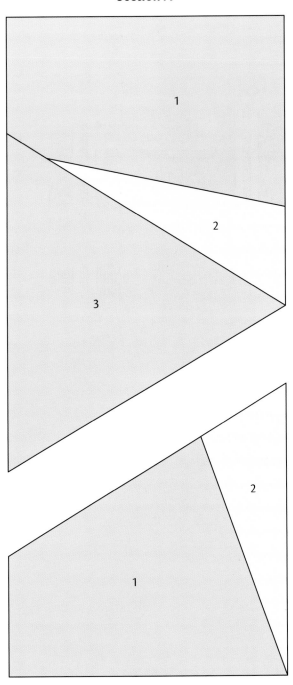

Section B

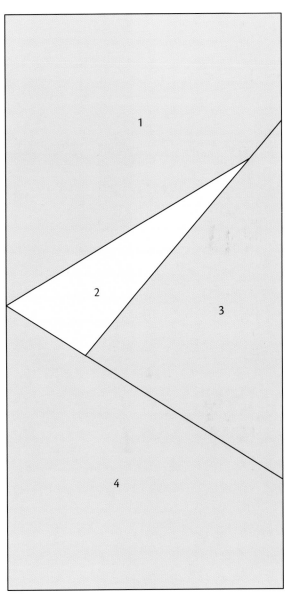

Section C

About the AUTHOR

Ellen Pahl has been making quilts for more than 20 years and has been editing books about making quilts for more than 15 years. She learned to sew as a child from her mother, who made most of their clothing. Quilts have always fascinated Ellen, and she made her first quilt in the early 1970s using typical dressmaking techniques and fabrics. Needless to say, she has learned a lot since then. As a freelance technical editor for various quilting and crafts book publishers, she feels fortunate to be able to work in a subject area that she loves.

Ellen belongs to a small quilting group that makes quilts for charity. She has also taught classes in hand appliqué and hand quilting. In addition to quilting, she enjoys gardening, cooking, basket weaving, and floral design. She lives in Coopersburg, Pennsylvania, with her family, two cats, and five chickens.

THERE'S MORE ONLINE!
Find more great books on quilting, knitting, crochet, and more at www.martingale-pub.com.